Spain

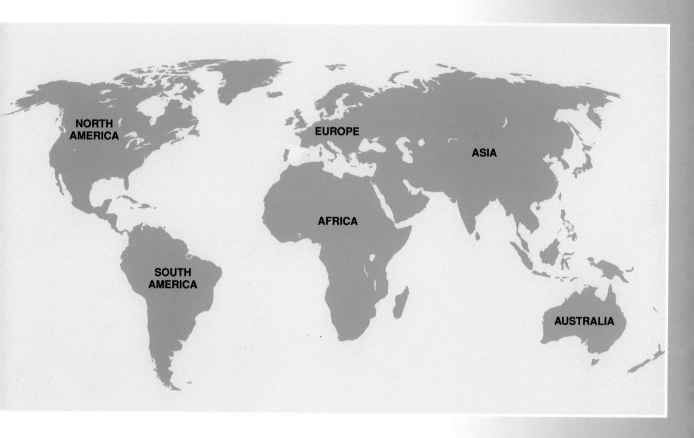

Clare Boast

Heinemann Interactive Library
Des Plaines, Illinois

Published by Heinemann Interactive Library,
an imprint of Reed Educational & Professional Publishing,
1350 East Touhy Avenue, Suit 240 West, Des Plaines, IL 60018

Produced by Times Offset (M) Sdn. Bhd.
Designed by AMR
Illustrations by Art Construction

02 01 00 99 98
10 9 8 7 6 5 4 3 2 1

Boast, Clare, 1965–
    Spain / Clare Boast
        p.   cm. – – (Next stop!)
    Includes bibliographical references and index.
    Summary: An introduction to the history, geography, culture, and modern daily life in Spain.
    ISBN 1-57572-570-3
    1. Spain – – Juvenile literature.   [1. Spain.]   I. Title.
II. Series.   97-16744
DP17. B58 1997   C I P
946 – – DC21   AC

Acknowledgments
The author and publisher are grateful to the following for permission to reproduce copyright photographs:
Aspect Picture Library Ltd. E. Mullis p.29; Trevor Clifford pp 10, 12–13, 14–15, 16–17, 19, 20, 21, 23, 25; Tony Stone Images R. Frerck p.7 (right); Trip R. Belbin p.26, D. Cumming pp.18, 22, M. Feeney pp.9, 11, 27, R. Gibbs p.7 (left), N. Ray p.8, H. Rogers p.4 (left), E. Smith pp.4 (right), 28, B. Turner p.24.

Cover photograph reproduced with permission of:
    background: Tony Stone Images, Owen Franken
    child: The Image Bank, L. Gordon.

Special thanks to Betty Root for her comments in the preparation of this book.

Words in the book in bold, **like this**, are explained in the glossary on page 31.

CONTENTS

INTRODUCTION

WHERE IS SPAIN?

Spain is in Europe, with France to the northwest. Spain and Portugal form a **peninsula** that is surrounded by three bodies of water: the Atlantic Ocean, the Bay of Biscay, and the Mediterranean Sea. The capital city of Spain is Madrid, where about three million people live.

This tower, in the city of Seville, was built about 1,000 years ago. People say the first builders covered it in a layer of gold.

A cathedral in Santiago de Compostela. Spain has many grand cathedrals.

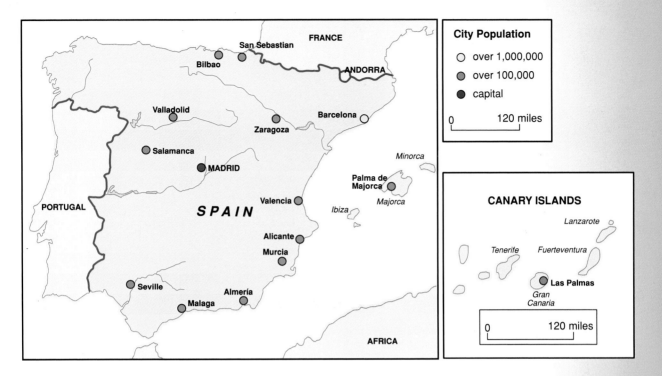

SPAIN'S HISTORY

Spain was part of the **Roman Empire** for about 600 years. In 711 A.D., Muslim Arabs, called Moors, captured Spain. It split into different warring kingdoms. In 1492, Spain became one country again, ruled by a king.

In 1930 there was a **civil war** in Spain. When the war ended in 1939, the king's army had lost. But in 1975, the Spanish people decided to have a king again. Now the king rules with a **government** chosen by the people.

Because Spain once was many different countries, there are still parts of Spain that have their own languages and traditions. Some people in these places would like to become separate from Spain again.

5

THE LAND

PLATEAUS AND MOUNTAINS

Most of Spain is high, fairly flat land—a plateau. The plateau is not all flat. It is split into two by mountains. Rivers flow across the plateau, making valleys. Some valleys have rich soil and are good for farming. The smaller rivers sometimes dry up in the summer.

Spain is separated from France by the Pyrenees mountains.

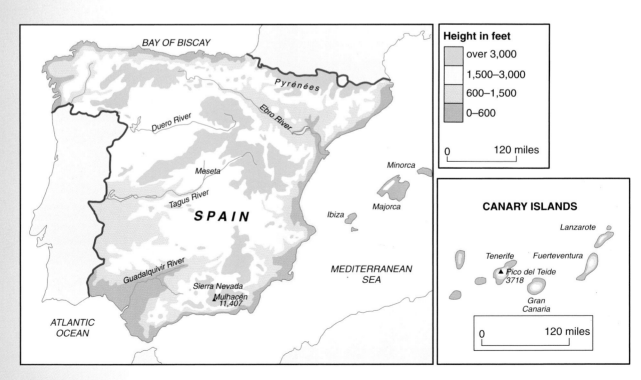

A volcano on Tenerife, in the Canary Islands. It has not erupted for a long time.

These windmills were once used to grind flour, or to pump water up from under the ground.

SPAIN'S ISLANDS

Spain owns several islands off its coast, as well as the Canary Islands, off the coast of northwest Africa. Many **tourists** go to these islands for vacations, as well as going to Spain itself.

Most of the Canary Islands are old **volcanoes**. The sand on some of the beaches is black, because it is old **lava** from the volcanoes, worn down by the sea. These islands are hot and fairly dry all year round.

Canary birds are named after the Canary Islands. They live there in the wild.

WEATHER, PLANTS, AND ANIMALS

The Costa del Sol (Sunshine Coast), on Spain's Mediterranean coast, has many hotels for **tourists**, who come for the good weather.

THE WEATHER

On the plateau, winters are very cold and summers are very hot. On the Atlantic **coast**, and in the north of Spain, it is wetter and cooler than on the plateau. The weather on the Mediterranean coast is somewhere between the two.

PLANTS AND ANIMALS

Different plants grow in different areas of Spain. Trees grow in the cool, wet mountains and in the north. In the hot, dry areas, only a few bushes and grass grow. These areas are called scrubland.

There are not many wild animals left in Spain. Some of them, like bears, wolves, wild cats, and wild boar are protected in **national parks**. Tarantula spiders are protected, too!

You could go to prison if you harm animals in any of Spain's five national parks.

The town of Alicante has scrubland all around it. A few orange and lemon trees grow there, too.

TOWNS AND CITIES

A **plaza** in the town of Caparossa. You can find squares like this in most Spanish towns and villages.

OLD TOWNS

Many of the towns and cities in Spain are very old. Some of them have walls built in the time of the **Roman Empire**.

There are many different kinds of buildings in the towns. They show how long the town has been lived in and what kinds of people lived there. Many towns and villages have buildings built by the Moors, like the Great Mosque in Cordoba, for example, and also by the people who came after them.

Alicante, in southern Spain, has grown from a small town into a tourist resort.

Barcelona has grown outside its city walls. It is a busy port, a tourist resort, and has many factories, too.

NEW BUILDING

Many old cities have grown outside their city walls. The old town centers are still very busy, though. Many of these towns are visited by **tourists**.

Tourists also go to the **coast**, especially to the islands and the Mediterranean coast. There are many new hotels, nightclubs, and restaurants to attract tourists.

11

LIVING IN VALENCIA

THE GRIJALVO FAMILY

Manuel and Cati Grijalvo live in an apartment in the city of Valencia. They have one boy, Manu, age twelve, and one girl, Begoña, age ten.

The family live in an apartment about half an hour's drive from the city center.

THE FAMILY'S DAY

Manuel and Cati work full-time. Cati works in an office at the university. Manuel works for a book publisher. They each have a car to get around easily. Manu and Begoña both go to the same school.

Manu plays soccer for the Serranos Football Club.

Begoña goes to ballet class after school.

MEALTIMES

The family can do their food shopping in the small stores near the apartment. There are lots of stores.

One of Cati's local stores. "Frutas y Verduras" means "Fruit and Vegetables".

The family are up early, at 6:30 A.M. They only have a small breakfast of coffee or hot chocolate and cookies. They have lunch at work or school.

The family eats their main meal at about 7:00 P.M. Manuel does not eat with them during the week. He often works late.

The family eating breakfast.

FARMING IN SPAIN

Farmland in northeast Spain. Wheat is growing in the fields.

DIFFERENT CROPS

The farmers in Spain grow all kinds of crops. They grow grapes in **vineyards** to make wine. They grow lemons, oranges, and olives for olive oil. The flat land of the plateau is good for growing wheat and barley. They keep sheep and goats for milk and meat. They raise pigs, too.

Spain is famous for making a special kind of wine called sherry.

HELPING CROPS GROW

The long, dry summers are a problem for farmers in most parts of Spain. Sometimes there is not enough rain for the crops, even in the winter. This is a problem the Moors faced, too, more than 1,000 years ago.

The answer to the problem, then and now, is **irrigation**. This means using water from rivers, **reservoirs**, or from underground. Ordinary farms use irrigation. So do the small farms that grow water-hungry vegetables, like tomatoes and melons.

A farmer checking his vines. He grows vegetables like sweetcorn and cabbages, too.

LIFE ON A FARM

THE MERINO FAMILY

Chelo Merino lives in an apartment in Marcilla in the north of Spain. She lives with her brother, Enrique, and her two sons, Javier, who is 19, and Manolo, who is 17.

The family and some friends in their apartment in Marcilla.

The family owns a farm near Marcilla. They keep bulls that are used for bullfighting and bull running, both popular sports in Spain. The bulls have to be fed special food to make them strong. They can be dangerous. Chelo's husband was killed by a bull a few years ago.

There are 300 bulls on the farm. They eat grass and bean stalks three times a day to grow strong.

The bulls are very valuable. The veterinarian comes to check that they are well.

THE FAMILY'S DAY

The family all works on their farm. The boys have worked there since they were 12. Everyone has breakfast at 7:00 A.M. and then goes to work on the farm. They work until 8:30 P.M., with a break for lunch.

MEALTIMES

The family eats all of their meals together. They go home to the village for lunch at about 2:00 P.M. They have their evening meal after they get back from the farm, at about 9:00 P.M. They eat meat, rice, vegetables, and fruit. They eat bread with almost every meal.

The family can get almost everything they need in the local stores.

SPANISH STORES

Spain used to be a very poor country. People did not have much money to spend. Now Spain is richer. One of the main reasons for this is the money made from **tourists**.

A supermarket in Barcelona. Supermarket shopping is quicker than shopping in small stores.

BIGGER STORES

One of the effects of people having more money to spend is that there are more stores that sell clothes, food, and other **goods** to Spanish people and tourists.

Even the food stores are bigger. Now busy shoppers can buy bread, cheese, cakes, vegetables, canned goods, and meat in supermarkets, rather than going to many different small stores.

Street bars and stalls in Valencia. You can find stalls like these in towns and cities all over Spain.

LOCAL STORES

People can still buy things from local stores and street markets, even in the cities. Many people prefer these stores to supermarkets. Fruit and vegetables in the markets, are often fresher, because they have come straight from local farms.

OPENING HOURS

Most shops open at 9:30 A.M., but some, especially bread stores, open earlier. Most stores close at about 2:00 P.M. They stay closed for the hottest part of the day. They open again at about 4:30 P.M. and stay open until about 8:00 P.M.

People in Spain, and many other hot countries, stop work to eat and rest in the early afternoon when it is very hot.

19

SPANISH FOOD

TRADITIONAL FOOD

There are many Spanish dishes that have been cooked using the same recipes for many years. They use foods that can be grown or caught locally. Paella uses seafood, meat, vegetables, and rice. Some recipes are suited to the weather. Gaspacho is a cold, spicy vegetable soup. It makes a good lunch in hot weather.

These people are eating paella straight from the pan it was cooked in.

These **tourists** are having a cold drink in a well-shaded bar.

TAPAS BARS

You can find tapas bars all over Spain.
Tapas are small snacks, served with a drink.
They are made from meat and vegetables.
Each bar makes its own special tapas.
Tapas stop people from getting hungry
between a small breakfast and a late
lunch, or between lunch and dinner.

MADE IN SPAIN

Spain sells **goods** to other countries, from food and drinks, to cars. Goods sold to other countries are called exports.

SOUVENIRS

Spain makes most of its money from **tourists**, who spend money in hotels and restaurants. They also buy **souvenirs** of their visits. Most of the lace and guitars made in Spain are sold to tourists.

These men are pouring Rioja wine into bottles. Wine is Spain's biggest export.

FACTORIES

There are many more factories in the cities and towns now than there were 30 years ago. They make clothes and cars. There are shipyards that build ships.

Spanish workers are paid lower wages than workers doing the same jobs in the rest of Europe. Companies find it cheaper to set up factories, or to send work to factories in Spain rather than having work done in their own country.

The U.S. car company, Ford, makes some of its cars in Spain, in Valencia.

About 2 million cars are made in Spain every year. That is one car every four minutes!

GETTING AROUND

Spain is improving its road, railroad, and sea travel because of the **tourist** industry. Airports are being modernized, too. But there are still places with narrow dirt roads in the less-visited parts of Spain.

RAILROAD

Madrid is the center of the railroad network. Fast trains run from there to all the big cities, like Seville and Barcelona. The trains that run from the cities to smaller places are slower and run less often.

Seville railroad station. Fast trains can go at 150 miles per hour.

Trams run on rail tracks in the road. They have their own routes and stopping places, just like buses.

The trams in Valencia run along the main roads.

ROADS

The road system in Spain spreads out from Madrid, just like the railroads. Even so, it is faster to travel by train. The train takes about three hours to reach Seville from Madrid. It takes about six hours by car. Also, you have to pay to drive on some highways.

The roads to the tourist resorts have been improved. They go to the edges of the resorts and then circle around them, to keep the traffic moving.

SPORTS AND VACATIONS

Soccer is a very popular sport in Spain. People like to play it, watch it on the TV, and at soccer stadiums.

BULLFIGHTING

Spanish people and **tourists** both go to see bullfights. Bullfighting has gone on in Spain for hundreds of years. A **matador** with a red cape fights a bull.

The bull chases the matador, who teases it with his cape. When it is tired, he kills it—unless it gets him first.

The new tourist hotels are built tall and close together, to fit in as many visitors as possible.

TIME OFF

People like to relax in cafés and bars, or go for walks in the cool evenings.

VACATIONS

Not many Spanish people leave Spain to go on vacation. Some of them go to the beaches on the **coast**. Some of them go to the country, some visit relatives, or go skiing in the mountains.

In some parts of Spain people play pelota, an old Spanish sport. You have to hit a ball against a wall until someone misses.

27

FESTIVALS AND ARTS

People in Jerez dress up for a horse fair, another traditional celebration.

FESTIVALS

Festivals are called fiestas in Spain. Many fiestas are religious. Most Spanish people are Catholic.

Most towns have their own saint who has a special saint's day. On this day, people say special prayers and parade through the streets singing and dancing. People who have been named after the saint receive presents.

SPECIAL DAYS

Some parades and feasts remember things that have happened in Spain in the past. People dress up and decorate the streets with flowers and lights.

People dressed up as Moors and Christians for this parade in **Seville**, to remember when they fought to control Spain.

FLAMENCO

The flamenco is a traditional Spanish **gypsy** dance. Dancers wear traditional clothes. The music is usually played on a guitar, sometimes with a singer, and gets faster and faster. The dancers go faster, too, stamping their feet and clicking their fingers.

Gypsies first came to Spain more than 500 years ago. They are proud of all their traditions, including flamenco dancing.

29

SPAIN FACT FILE

People
People from Spain are called Spaniards.

Capital city
The capital city is Madrid. Madrid is in the center of Spain.

Largest cities
Madrid is the largest city with about 3 million people. The second largest is Barcelona, and the third largest is Valencia.

Head of country
The head of Spain is a king, but the country is run by a **government**.

Population
There are about 40 million people living in Spain.

Money
The money in Spain is called the peseta.

Language
People speak Spanish. Spanish is one of the most widely spoken languages in the world.

Education
Children have to go to school from the age of 6 to 16.

MORE BOOKS TO READ

Butler, Daphne. *Spain*. Austin, TX: Raintree Steck-Vaughn, 1993.
Wright, Nicola. *Getting to Know: Spain and Spanish*. Hauppauge, NY: Barron's, 1993.

GLOSSARY

civil war This is when citizens of one country fight each other.

coast This is where the land meets the sea.

goods These are things people have made.

government These are people who run the country. In Spain the government is chosen by the people.

gypsies These are traveling people who came from India, but have spread all over the world.

irrigation This means watering the land

lava This is melted rock from below the Earth's surface.

matador This is a bullfighter.

national park This is an area of land that belongs to the government and is left wild.

peninsula This is a piece of land with water almost all around it.

plaza This is an open square in a town, often with stores around the edges.

reservoirs These are manmade lakes made to store water.

Roman Empire The Romans were people from Rome in Italy, who took over much of Europe and other parts of the world from 750 B.C. to 300 A.D.

souvenir This is something that reminds someone of a place they have been to.

tourist This is someone who visits a place on vacation.

vineyards These are where grapes grow.

volcano This is a mountain that sometimes throws out melted rock or ash.

INDEX